What This Book Will Do for You

By the time you've finished reading this book, you will be better able to make tough decisions. You'll be able to recognize the basic issues involved in the decisions, take the long view with regard to consequences, identify the real problems, involve other people, and weigh your own options.

Other Titles in the Successful Office Skills Series

Making
TOUGH
DECISIONS

Donald H. Weiss

American Management Association

New York • Atlanta • Boston • Chicago • Kansas City • San Francisco • Washington, D.C.
Brussels • Toronto • Mexico City

This publication is designed to provide accurate and authoritative
information in regard to the subject matter covered. It is sold with
the understanding that the publisher is not engaged in rendering
legal, accounting, or other professional service. If legal advice or
other expert assistance is required, the services of a competent professional person should be sought.

Library of Congress Cataloging-in-Publication Data

Weiss, Donald H., 1936–
    Making tough decisions / Donald H. Weiss.
        p.   cm. — (The successful office skills series)
    Includes bibliographical references and index.
    ISBN 0-8144-7821-2
    1. Decision-making.   I. Title.   II. Series.
    HD30.23.W448   1993
    658.4'03—dc20   93-4121
                                                    CIP

Printing number

10   9   8   7   6   5   4   3   2   1

CONTENTS

Decisions, decisions, decisions. All the time, decisions. Seems that making decisions is all we ever do. Some are easier than others, such as, ''Hmm, what should I eat for lunch?'' Others are quite a bit more difficult, such as, ''Should I hire George or Jeffrey?''

We'll spend our time together talking about the decisions most people would agree are relatively tough to make—including business decisions that people are making even as you read this sentence, decisions like these:

> Should I fire the employee whose performance isn't up to standard?
> Who on my staff should I lay off to meet management's demand for a 10 percent reduction?
> Should I follow this career or that one?
> Should I accept this position or that one?
> Should I quit my job?
> Should I go into business for myself?

Or personal decisions like these:

> Should I get married?
> Should I have children?
> Should I buy a house?
> Should I get a divorce?
> Should I go to college?
> Should I go to graduate school?
> Should I go into the military?

You may want to add a few to the list—health-related decisions (for example, an elective surgery), purchase decisions (maybe a new car), and so on—but the questions in the lists require pretty tough decisions in anyone's book. No sure-fire method exists that will guarantee that you make right and proper choices, but I do have some steps for you to follow and some tools that you can use that will make it easier to make tough decisions.

First, take the long view; that is, decide what's important to you—not just in the context of the specific decision you have to make, but rather in the context of your life in general or of your business life in particular. Second, approach decision making as you would problem solving; after all, no decision is difficult unless it involves a problem. Third, involve other people when it's appropriate. Fourth, examine and weigh alternatives, using decision trees or other devices for guiding your thinking. Tough decisions demand tough means by which to make them.

CHAPTER ONE

Identifying the Basic Issues

✍

Often, what makes a decision tough is that you haven't identified what really is at stake. You ask,

What should I do? This or that? Instead, you should be asking, What will happen if I decide to do this, rather than that? Why do I have to make this decision at all—to what end? What or who will be affected by my making this decision, and how? Making tough decisions requires that you develop a context in which you identify assumptions and beliefs, attitudes, values, goals, and objectives.

Grappling With the Basics

I'm going to let two brothers—Tobin and Sid— illustrate how you go about making tough decisions. They're not real people, but they have to grapple with real issues.

I'm going to present the brothers in a dialogue/discussion format. This is an excellent way to address tough decisions. Dialogue provides discussion with depth and substance. Discussion compares opinions or perspectives, often merely for the purpose of getting someone else to accept your point of view, and also helps people get their ideas into the open.

Dialogue examines opinions and perspectives and results in clarifying relations. Participants in a dialogue ask each other questions that probe beneath the surface of an opinion, an idea, a thought, a value, or an attitude. They push each other to consider the implications of what they're seeing in ways that discussion omits. There's nothing new in this format; Plato taught us how to do it over 2,000 years ago.

When balanced against one another and when they work together, dialogue and discussion allow for a healthy give-and-take that produces a new perspective built out of elements of the old ones. And, although it's possible to hold both discussions and dialogues with yourself, it's much more fruitful to hold them with someone else—especially if you have to meet the demands of two or more perspectives at the same time.

When you're reading this book, ask yourself if you've been doing what these brothers do. If you haven't been probing and taking the steps they do, ask, "What can I do to adopt their methods?"

The Brothers' Dilemmas

Both Tobin and his older brother Sid feel impaled on the horns of separate and different dilemmas. Tobin has two job offers, and he'd love to take them both. Sid, on the other hand, can't decide between spending a considerable amount of time coaching one of his employees and letting him go. On a Sunday afternoon, out on Sid's patio, they talk about their concerns.

Sid: I wish I had your problem. Choosing between two good jobs shouldn't be so difficult.

Tobin: I don't know about that. I want them both. They're not much alike, either. The marketing support job is with a pretty big company—international owners, a couple of billion dollars a year in revenues. It doesn't pay as much as I want, but they're talking about fast advancement and growth. The other one, as an account ex-

Sid: ecutive in a printing company, pays more. I'd have more freedom. I'd also get a shot at being a sales manager in a couple of years when the man who would be my boss retires.

Sid: Well, which makes more sense to your career plan?

Tobin: They both make perfect sense. The downside of the first is that I'd be a small fish in an awfully big pond. The downside of the other one is that I'd probably peak early. After sales manager, I'd not have too many places to go in the smaller company. I'd have to look for a bigger job elsewhere. You seem to have something on your mind, too.

Sid: Yeah. Something at work, that's all.

Tobin: Can I help?

Sid: I have to make a decision, too. About an experienced employee—George—who's having trouble adapting to some new equipment. He's great in manual operations, but he's not cutting it on the new computer. A literacy problem, I think. We don't have any place else we can use him, either. It'll take a lot of time to coach him through the problem, but he's been too valuable just to dump out. I have to do something about it tomorrow.

Tobin: I have to give both companies an answer tomorrow, too.

The brothers sit quietly, neither one quite sure if he can help the other make his tough decision—

in spite of the fact that Sid has started a line of questioning that both need to follow: "Which makes more sense to your career plan?"

Tobin needs to answer that question, and Sid needs to take a cue from it, as well. How does coaching or firing the employee fit in with his long-term plans for the unit? Placing a tough decision into a context, where you can examine your assumptions and beliefs, attitudes and values, and goals and objectives takes some of the toughness out of the decision.

Context

Some writers call it a *mental model*, others call it a *paradigm*. Whatever you call it, your context is the slant you have on things, your perspective or frame of reference. It's how you look at the world, judge what's real or unreal, true or false, good or bad, right or wrong, important or unimportant, beautiful or ugly. In the vernacular, a context is "where you're coming from."

Assumptions and Beliefs: Everyone grows up learning a set of unquestioned beliefs from the surrounding culture or social group. Beliefs may include the concept that the earth produces day and night by rotating on its axis or the conviction that financial growth and the pursuit of happiness mean the same thing. You usually take these mental building blocks for granted and don't give them much thought—until you're faced with a tough decision.

Many of your beliefs are based on experience, but often you fall back on a limited set of experiences to support them. For example, a person might have had contact with a few people of a particular minority group or religious denomination; he then draws the hasty conclusion that he knows all about *those* people. "Oh, yeah. I've had a couple of them working for me. Not very good workers, really. Come in late. Don't get much work done. Yeah, I know all about them." And so another prejudice is born, and decisions are made on the basis of the bias, rather than on the basis of facts.

These assumptions and beliefs form a body of knowledge against which you measure new ideas. Usually, if new ideas fit with your preexisting body of knowledge, you say they're true and the objects to which they refer are real. Similarly, if they don't fit, you throw out the new ideas. Galileo, because his ideas about the solar system didn't fit with the Roman Catholic church's Aristotelian notion that the heavens rotated around the earth, was convicted of heresy and forced to recant his views. His perspective on the solar system, which today we take for granted, only recently (historically speaking) gained universal popularity.

Attitudes and Values: Your willingness to make decisions and act on them depends upon how you feel about the issues and upon your readiness to respond to issues in certain ways—in other words, your attitudes. Many of your attitudes have been acquired the same way your assumptions and beliefs were: through social learning and limited experience. Values—beliefs concerning good and bad, right and wrong, beautiful and ugly—are also usually learned at your parents' and teachers' feet. They undergird your attitudes and the decisions you make.

Values determine the importance of beliefs and actions. For example, for some people, it's okay to destroy a rain forest in return for economic gain. For others, it's not. For some people, it's okay to discriminate against older employees "because they're not as flexible as younger people." For others, it's not. For some people it's okay to overcharge customers to improve cash flow. For others, it's not. You make decisions concerning these options on the basis of your prevailing values, many of which can change with time and circumstances but most of which are relatively fixed and stable.

Sometimes people act on their organization's values even if they don't necessarily agree with them (or don't agree with them all of the time). That's the basis of expediency.

Sid: If I let George go, I'll meet my budget requirements faster, even though I know George will suffer for it.

Sometimes people express one set of values (so-called espoused values) but act on another set. We see that in supervisory and management training all the time. The trainees go back to work infused with benevolent intentions to be warmer, friendlier, and fairer, only to see their intentions go by the board at the first sign of a crisis. Decisions are often made on the basis of which of competing values produce the greatest immediate payoff.

Goals and Objectives: The payoffs you get from your decisions and your actions actually drive your choices. You elect to do those things that yield desired results. Profits, market leadership, growth and development—these are the goals that drive any business, and the business decisions you make at any level of the organization should serve one or more of these goals. You have to ask yourself, when confronted with a tough decision, "How will my choices contribute to or take away from my ability to help the organization satisfy its vision and its mission—that is, meet its goals?"

A much wider range of goals and payoffs drives your personal decisions, and you will get a chance to work on your own payoffs later. Everything you do, all the choices you make, are motivated by desires, wishes, or needs. Just as you usually take your assumptions and beliefs, your attitudes and values, for granted, so too you rarely question your motives, or drives—until you're faced with a tough decision.

The combined elements of the contexts in which you live and work form an interdependent fabric of choices, a system in which a choice in one part of the system affects the outcomes in other parts. These elements are the basic issues that ultimately make a decision tough or easy.

CHAPTER TWO

Taking the Long View

We can separate the basic beliefs, values, attitudes, goals, and objectives that drive decisions into seven dimensions of any person's life.* And that's not merely for convenience either; anything falling outside of those categories is probably inconsequential. The seven dimensions are:

1. Personal values (e.g., health)
2. Family relations
3. Career
4. Finances
5. Material goods
6. Social relations
7. Community relations

Goals and Objectives

The defining characteristic of a dimension is a set of closely related goals and objectives. A goal con-

*Adapted from Donald H. Weiss, *Get Organized! How to Control Your Life Through Self-Management* (New York: AMACOM, 1986), and Donald H. Weiss, *Managing Stress* (New York: AMACOM, 1987) (Successful Office Skills Series) and from *Get Organized! for Windows: The Goal-Driven Personal and Performance Manager for Busy People* (St. Louis: Self-Management Communications, 1992), the author's adaptation (with Randy Wilp) of these ideas for PC users.

sists of a target—something of value that you want, a result or a payoff that you want to get from the things that you do. For example, one of Tobin's career goals is "Become sales manager within two years." One of his material goods goals is "Build a new four-bedroom house next year." And one of his community relations goals is "Get elected to the school board within the next five years."

An objective is a step along the path toward achieving a goal; it's an intermediate goal or a milestone, a means toward an end. A sample of an objective is "Save $15,000 next year as a down payment on the new house." In and by itself, an objective doesn't mean much; it takes on importance only as it relates to the goal or goals that drive it.

All the decisions you make and all the actions you take to execute those decisions serve to satisfy the demands of one or more of these dimensions. If a decision or an action doesn't satisfy your own demands, you feel uncomfortable, ill at ease with what you're doing. If a decision you make in one dimension interferes with the demands of another dimension, you feel the same discomfort or unease. It's very difficult to live a contradiction. Psychologists call it cognitive or emotional dissonance.

Figure 2-1 details the contents of these seven dimensions. The descriptions in each box will help you identify your own goals in each dimension; you can decide for yourself your most important goals.

Figure 2-1. Dimensions of a whole person.

Personal Values	Family Relations	Career
The quality of health you wish to maintain, the degree of literacy and awareness you want to reach, the spiritual values important to you.	The kinds of relationships you want to have with your relatives (e.g., your immediate family, your spouse).	Work-related activities; how you want to earn your income, and the status in your profession that you want to achieve.

Finances	Material Goods	Social Relations	Community Relations
The amount of money you would like to earn at different stages of your life and over the course of your lifetime.	The types of things you want to own (e.g., a house, automobiles, furniture, clothing).	The kinds of relationships you wish to have with people other than your family (e.g., with friends and acquaintances).	The status you wish to achieve where you live (e.g., becoming an elected official or a volunteer leader in church or synagogue).

Adapted from Donald H. Weiss, *Get Organized! for Windows: The Goal-Driven Personal and Performance Manager for Busy People* (St. Louis: Self-Management Communications, 1992), and other SOS books.

Taking in the Whole Picture

Every decision—large and life-changing or small but important—fits into a context of assumptions, beliefs, attitudes, values, goals, and objectives, all woven together into a system of related life dimensions. Each decision you make constitutes a choice from a complex set of elements in your context that affects not only the immediate issues or circumstances but many other decisions yet to come and that may not come for a number of years.

Life-changing decisions and small but important decisions alike require that you consider the context that surrounds them. The context itself then determines the limits of the inquiry you have to make. Tobin's considerations have a much broader scope, with longer-term issues, than do Sid's.

Life-Changing Decisions: For Tobin, the question his brother asked—"Which makes more sense to your career plan?"—should lead him to consider what's important to him within the seven dimensions of his life. He then can make his decision in relation to the goals he has set for himself in the career and financial dimensions. His choices now may affect his family, social, and community relations, not only now but far into the future.

Tobin: I like the fact that I could get ahead faster in the international corporation, but it's going to mean a lot of travel. I'll probably have to relocate several times over the next six or eight years.

Sid: So?

Tobin: You know Jane wouldn't want to uproot the kids that often. Besides, I've been active with school affairs here, and I'm pretty well known in town. I might consider running for school board in a couple of years. All that would go up in smoke if I had to relocate.

Sid: And with the other job?

Tobin: That's a lot of travel, too, but more around the area than overseas, and there'd be no relocation involved.

Sid: You know, Jane might not agree. The kids are young. They'd adjust pretty well in new places. Learn a second or third language easily, too. Travel's educational.

Tobin: I know that, but, still. . . .

Tobin will have to take a long hard look at what's important to him. Notice that the conversation focuses on family and community goals. The dialogue shows clearly how the decisions he makes now could radically affect decisions he *and* his family will make in the future.

If you have a similar decision to make, you should look at your goals and objectives and at the values that drive you. Your objectives and decisions should be associated with at least one of those goals or values. If they are not, they could become barriers to achieving goals. Listing your goals can help you identify when and where goals conflict with one another.

For example, Tobin might have a family relations goal like this one:

Become closer with the children by spending more time with them every day.

At the same time, he has a career goal that says:

Become a sales manager by the end of two years by working longer hours every day.

The conditions listed in these goals could be barriers to accomplishing either goal.

Tangible and Intangible Goals: Goals exhibit two very different qualities: tangibility and intangibility. In the dialogue, Tobin talked about tangible goals—income, career moves—things you can experience with your senses. Later, he focused on relatively intangible goals—family values, community relationships—payoffs that satisfy emotional needs. Both types of goals are payoffs that people seek from their efforts, and, although they are not mutually exclusive, sometimes one type of goal can outweigh the other.

People often have difficulty integrating their goals. For example, they may sacrifice intangible payoffs (such as family relationships) for tangible ones (more and more income). They also have difficulty seeing that, sometimes, tangible and intangible goals can support one another or lead to one or another. For example, most career goals are linked to financial goals; achieving financial goals can lead to improved family and community relationships, as well as to acquiring more material goods. On top of it all, achieving all your tangible goals can lead to the intangible payoff of increased self-esteem.

Questions that Tobin should be answering and that reveal the context in which he has to make his decision are listed in the accompanying box.

To help you sort out your goals, do the paper and pencil exercise in the Appendix of this book before continuing with your reading.

Making Major Decisions

Finding out what drives him might help Tobin, but Sid's problem is different. It's not life-changing for him, that is, his decision probably will not affect his entire life (although it may be life-changing for George, the other person affected).

A Context for Making a Decision

- How does a given decision fit into the total picture of my goals and objectives?
- How would a decision one way or another affect those goals and my ability to achieve them?
- Who else would be affected, and how?
- What would be the positive and negative consequences of inaction, that is, if I didn't make any choice at all and left things as they are?
- What would be the positive and negative consequences of doing something, regardless of what action I took?

However, it's a major decision, because whatever course of action he chooses will affect other people, his work unit, and his company. He has to make his choice in the context of the big picture that directs all those lives. He has some important questions to answer, too, in order to identify his context for making this decision.

Tobin: What would happen if you fired that guy?

Sid: I'd lose a man who knows everything there is to know about our business. He's been in it for ten years—since he graduated high school. Besides, he's got a family to support.

Tobin: He graduated high school, so where's the literacy problem?

Sid: A diploma's no guarantee of literacy in either reading or math, brother. He can read most things, but that operator's manual's tough stuff. He makes a good try at it, but he can't get past the basics, can't do the more sophisticated operations the job requires.

Tobin: How important is the computer? He got along very well without it before, from the looks of things.

Sid: That was then. This is now. Productivity and quality demands have changed. He can't keep up.

Tobin: What's the company's position on this sort of thing?

Sid: I put him on performance notice at his last quarterly review. He knows what he has to do, but he hasn't been able to measure up yet.

Tobin: No, you missed my point. What does the company *want* you to do?

Sid: Policy? We espouse loyalty to employees, but we also demand high standards. The bottom line overrides loyalty as a major issue.

Tobin: What would happen if you took the time to work with the guy more?

Sid: My personal productivity would fall off, and the other guys might get a bit ticked that I'm spending so much time with one person.

Tobin: Can you afford that?

Sid: No, but hell, Tobe. He's a great guy and knows the job. I'd hate to hurt his family, too.

Tobin: Business and sentimentality don't always mix.

Sid: That's why I'm having a problem with this. If I let him go, my bottom line will suffer anyway. Recruiting someone new, interviewing, selecting, training, coaching—that'll all take time and money. Since we hired him ten years ago, his base salary is lower than what I'll have to pay someone now.

Tobin has been talking his brother through the steps any supervisor has to take when considering what to do with a nonperforming employee. Following this process, you arrive at the question "What do I do with this person?" only after you have answered many other questions, including "What is company policy with regard to nonperforming employees?" and "How does coaching this person fit with the overall plan of the organization? With the big picture?" Then you funnel down, answering some of the questions that Tobin asked Sid to examine. These are listed in the next box.

As you see, Sid's questions are similar to Tobin's. He doesn't have to review all his drivers to make the decision, but he has to review all the conditions of his role as supervisor. Then the consequences of his decision, whatever it may turn out to be, will become clear.

Job-Related Big-Picture Questions

- What is the problem?
- How does it affect you and your responsibilities, other people and their responsibilities, and the organization as a whole?
- What are the company's policies and procedures with respect to this type of problem?
- What would happen if you didn't do anything?
- What are the positive and negative consequences of inaction?
- What are the positive and negative consequences of taking some kind of action, regardless of what action you take?

Looking at the big picture is a major step toward making a tough decision, but it's only one of several big steps. Next, you have to identify the real problem before you can decide how to solve it.

CHAPTER THREE

The Five Basic Steps in Solving Problems

❧

Tough decisions always involve a problem to solve. You wouldn't be faced with a dilemma unless things weren't quite the way you wanted them. That doesn't mean that something's *wrong*. Rather, it means that you have looked at what is and decided that it's not what you want.

Once you identify the essential issues—beliefs, attitudes, values, or goals—involved in making your tough decision, you have to zero in on the problem or problems creating the dilemma. Why aren't Tobin and Sid able to choose between one job and the other or retaining and firing the employee? Both men are capable, well-educated people. Why can't they make their decisions?

Tobin: I guess I just don't understand what your
problem is.

Sid: I guess I'm in the same boat with yours.

Symptoms Versus Causes

In fact, neither man really understands his *own*
problems yet—which points out how essential it
is that you identify your real problem before you
can solve it. How difficult this can be is illustrated
in a brief exchange between Tobin and Sid.

Tobin: What's your problem?

Sid: George can't keep up.

Tobin: No, that's his problem. What's yours?

Sid: What to do with him?

Tobin: No, that's the decision you have to make.
The problem's something else.

Most people look at the surface of their situation and call what they see the problem—when,
in reality, they're seeing only the results or the
symptoms of the actual problem. This is much like
going to the doctor with a pain in your shoulder
and being satisfied with a prescription for pain-
killers. You may not feel the pain once you've
taken the pills, but whatever caused the pain in
the first place will make its continued presence
known as soon as the effects of the pills wear off.
It may take time, tests, and X-rays, but you'll not
really stop the pain until you identify its cause—
the real problem—and deal with it.

Problem Identification

Identifying the real problem takes the guesswork
out of decision making. These five steps can help

you make the leap from a fuzzy guess to a more confident probability.

How to Identify a Problem

1. Collect initial data.
2. Formulate an initial statement.
3. Collect more data.
4. Identify associated factors.
5. Restate the problem.

Sometimes you may be able to jump from step 2 to step 5, but that's rare.

1. *Collect initial data.* You can express everything you do in terms of what things would be like in an ideal world—in terms of what should be. Your vision of your goals, standards, or objectives becomes the measure against which you compare current conditions and your possibilities (alternatives) for action.

Here's another analogy. Let's say you want to drive to a town fifty miles away from where you are. Knowing your destination is the starting point. You need to know where you want to go in order to arrive there and to decide on the best way to get there.

Sid: Okay, what would be the perfect situation for you?

Tobin: That's pretty easy. Do the things I want.

Sid: Like what?

Tobin: Make enough money to build the new house we've been talking about. The one we're in is too small. Oh, sure, Jane'll keep working. She's creating a career for herself, too, you know. That'll help build the new house. And, yeah, that's another thing to consider with the travel and relocation—Jane's work.

Sid: And?

Tobin: Like I said, I'd like to get into local politics. That's important to me. And the kids—their school and all. Yeah, I know what you said about travel being educational, but what about stability? I'd like to see the kids develop a stable and—what can I call it—a normal life.

Tobin is weaving the fabric of the context in which he has to make his choice. Moving from the ideal to the real is the next part of the data-collecting process. That the real doesn't match the ideal is a sure sign a problem exists.

Sid: How are things now? With your current job?

Tobin: Nowhere city. The pay's poor, the hours are long, the future's dim. No, I definitely need to take one of these two other jobs. How about you? What would be your ideal situation?

Sid: The personal time and the budget for keeping George on the job.

Tobin: Reality?

Sid: I have neither.

2. *Formulate the initial statement.* Once you have clearly separated what should be from what is, you can formulate an initial statement of the problem as the relationship between what should be and what is.

Sid: The brutal reality is that we don't have the time right now or the money in the budget to give George the retraining he needs to stay on the job.

Tobin: My brutal reality is that, unless I change jobs, I won't be able to do the things I think are right for my family. To compound the difficulty, the two job possibilities I have may create barriers to what I want.

3. *Collect additional data.* To identify your problem, you have to go beyond recognizing that what is doesn't match what you want. You need to know more about your situation.

For example, Sid's problem seems to be how to keep George in spite of a lack of funds and personal time to help him. But why has this become an issue? In short, here is the place for Sid to answer the questions why? what? when? who? where? and how?

Tobin: What happens with George in the course of a week?

Sid: Every order involves different settings on the machinery. The computer we installed makes those settings more accurately than a human being can, but you have to know how to program the computer. And the software's a little like a spreadsheet and involves some equations.

Tobin: When does George run into a problem with this, and how often does it happen?

Sid: George has to program new settings five, maybe six, times a day, and, almost every time he has to stop to compute a new setting, he runs into the same roadblock.

Tobin: Which is?

Sid: Filling in the right equation.

Tobin: Who besides George is affected by this?

Sid: Almost everyone. The time it takes George to set up his equipment and correct errors slows the entire process, not just for us, but for other units that interface with us.

Tobin: Hmm. Another question. Is this happening anyplace else in the unit or in similar units?

Sid [*after thinking about it for a few seconds*]: It could be.

Tobin: Where?

Sid: As I think about it, it seems like it happens all through the unit and anywhere else similar equipment's been installed. No one's output is like it was. People seem to be working harder just to stay even or to catch up on their quotas with the new equipment. George's situation is just much more pronounced and obvious.

Somewhere along the path of this inquiry, Sid may find both the immediate cause of George's problem and therefore the cause of Sid's dilemma. Just discovering these causes may suggest the solution to both George's and Sid's situations. The obvious dilemma Sid is facing may not tell the whole story, after all.

In Tobin's situation, the why, what, when,

who, where, and how questions concern his present job and each of the other potential jobs.

Tobin: When it comes down to it, I have a lot of questions to answer for myself. Why do I want to change jobs? What about the new jobs appeals to me and what doesn't? Who would benefit from the change, and how, for each position? Who would lose from the change, and how? Where should this problem be discussed, and with whom? Is it possible that the other people who factor into the equation have some answers for me?

Answering these questions could lead to discoveries similar to the one his brother has made.

4. *Identify contributing factors.* As you answer the questions posed in step 3, you can identify factors that contribute to the discrepancy between what is and what should be.

Sid: The more I think about this, the more I think we've been doing something very wrong. Like I said, George really isn't the only one having problems with the changeover. His is the worst performance, but everyone else's has slipped, too. Maybe we upgraded too fast and without the proper training.

Tobin: What training did you get?

Sid: Oh, I was sent to school to learn how to operate the equipment.

Tobin: Then?

Sid: I trained everyone else. An hour a day for a week.

Tobin: You went to school for how long?

Sid: Three solid days, but I have to know a lot more about the equipment than they do.

Tobin: Maybe you have to give George—and everyone else—more time.

Sid: It could be.

By following the steps I've outlined, Sid and Tobin may have come up with an important answer to an important question: How did George fall so far behind?

Tobin has a new way of looking at his dilemma as well.

Tobin: I think my real problem lies in what I want for the family, not just for myself, and for the long term, not just for the short. I think my dilemma's a question of setting priorities among my wishes.

5. *Make your final statement of the problem.* Both Sid and Tobin are in a position to restate their problems as the relationship between what is happening and the contributing factors. On the basis of that statement, they'll be able to list the alternative solutions to their problems.

Sid: Okay. George is falling so far behind because he learns slower than the other people, but the other people are not up to standard, either. This could be a function of their training.

Tobin: Could be. For my part, I may be looking at the wrong priorities for making my decisions. I need to look at how the positions would satisfy what Jane, the kids, and I want from the work I do.

There is never only one way to solve a problem or make a decision. These five basic steps, only a starting place for your inquiry, amount to detective work. Creativity begins where the detective work ends.

CHAPTER FOUR

Meeting Multiple Demands

❧

In a totally self-contained ideal world in which making a tough decision boils down to doing what you think you have to do, should do, or want to do, you identify the key issues and the causes of the problem and go on with your life. But who lives in a self-contained ideal world?

Everyone lives in a world populated by other people with needs, wishes, and requirements that intersect with ours. No one context exists separate and apart from all others. So how do you solve your problems when the decisions are not altogether yours to make?

Interlocking Contexts

Every context overlaps others. You can grasp this by drawing two interlocking circles and shading the area in which they overlap each other (Figure 4-1).

Circle A represents your context (e.g., in Sid's case, the context in which he has to make the decision whether to let George go). Circle B represents a second but related context (in Sid's case, his work group). Tobin's circle A represents the context of his decision of which job to accept, circle B represents his wife's. The shaded area, where the two circles overlap, represents where the two contexts flow together. Here's where the goals and objectives of two contexts coincide, for example, and can't be taken for granted.

Tobin: Jane's career is just getting established here. I'd better not take a job that would interfere with that.

Figure 4-1. Two interlocking contexts.

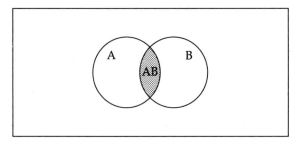

Sid: Is that what Jane said?

Tobin: Well, no. I haven't really discussed this with her to that extent.

Sid: It seems like a pretty good idea to do that. Map out a common strategy. Jane may see a move to be in her interest, too. You seem willing to stay put to meet her need; maybe she's willing to move to meet yours. A move might meet a common or shared need.

Tobin: I should be talking with the kids, too—but at six and nine, they're pretty young and flexible.

Sid: You could at least find out how they'd feel about leaving their school and their friends.

If you have to consider more than two contexts, the way both Tobin and Sid do, your picture might look Figure 4-2. Circle A represents Tobin's, circle B his wife's, and circle C his children's (assuming that they're pretty much the same). For Sid, circle A represents his, circle B the work unit's, and circle C the company's.

Figure 4-2. Three interlocking contexts.

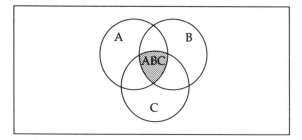

Sid: The unit's falling way below its production requirements, and management's breathing down my neck. They're saying speed it up, and, because George's figures are so low, they're saying he's the problem. They're saying let him go if he can't get up to speed on his own.

Tobin: You don't agree?

Sid: Not after what we've come up with here. But it's my neck if I don't turn things around.

Tobin: What's in your best interest?

Sid: I'm not sure just yet.

Tobin: The unit's?

Sid: Get everyone, including George, up to standard.

Tobin: The company's?

Sid: I think it's in the company's interest to add another week of training and to send George for some remedial reading and arithmetic. He can get it at the community college on his own time.

Tobin: Would that meet George's needs?

Sid: I think so. At this point, I think all our needs would be met this way.

Sid has just pointed out that his context overlaps more than two others. His picture actually comprises four different but related contexts—his own, George's, the unit's, and the company's—each of which has several life dimensions to satisfy, dimensions that sometimes come into odds with one another (see Figure 4-3). In another case involving four contexts—the struggle for survival

Figure 4-3. Four interlocking contexts.

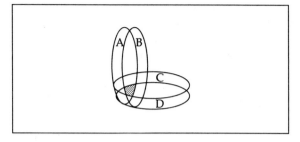

of the airline giant TWA—the conflicts between the several unions, the creditors, and former chairman Carl Icahn clearly illustrate how the demands in areas A, B, C, and D (the Pilots' Association, the Attendants' Union, the creditors, and Icahn) can totally overshadow the small common area shared by all four contexts.

It's difficult to diagram more than four interlocking contexts, but by now you should have a pretty good picture of what I'm talking about. It's not the picture that matters, but the concept. As John Donne said, "No man [or woman] is an island."

When to Involve Other People

You make tough decisions tougher if you try to make them by yourself even though other people are involved. You need to know when to include others in the process and when to make decisions alone. In the box, I list when it's probably not necessary to involve others.

When Not to Involve Other People

1. When the decision affects only you.
2. When you do not have time to consult with others and have to make the decision immediately.
3. When you're as competent as anyone else to make the decision and no other reason exists to involve someone else.

The next box lists conditions under which it is best to involve other people.

Three of the seven reasons for involving other people relate to gaining support for and commitment to the decision; three others relate to promoting effective decisions. You can express this relationship as an equation.

To put numbers to that proposition, let's rate the quality of information and the level of acceptance on a scale of 1 to 10, with 1 the lowest possible score and 10 the highest. Then:

> If the quality of the information underlying the decision is 0, the quality of the decision is equal to 0 even if the level of acceptance is 10.

Conversely,

> If the quality of the information is 10 but the level of acceptance is 0, then the quality of the decision is also 0.

When to Involve Other People

1. When the decision affects at least one other person.*
2. When you don't have the knowledge or skill.
3. To promote acceptance of the decision by other people, to maintain group cohesion or morale, or to gain commitment to executing the decision.
4. To promote acceptance of the decision by people outside your immediate group (e.g., upper management) if you need their support.
5. To get support for or help in training related to the decision.
6. To reduce the risk that the decision will lead to failure.
7. To improve the quality of your decision.

On the other hand,

If the quality of the information is 10 and the level of acceptance is 10, then the quality of the decision equals 100—and the probability that the decision you make is correct and will succeed is 100 percent as well.

*In a situation such as the one Sid confronts, you have to make the decision whether to let George go by yourself. Although you might consult with George about the causes of the problem, the final decision is yours and yours alone.

The Quality of a Decision

The quality of a decision is equal to the quality of the information that underlies the decision multiplied by the degree of its acceptance by the people responsible for carrying it out.

Tobin and Sid have both come to recognize the validity of this equation, and as they talk, they arrive at several new conclusions.

Tobin: I guess I should have talked with Jane about it before this. We talked about it some, but I never asked how it would affect her down the road if we had to relocate—especially if we had to relocate overseas.

Sid: That surprises me, and it surprises me that she didn't give you feedback right then.

Tobin: I don't think she realizes that relocation could be required.

Sid: Probably not. Just like I don't think upper management realizes that we may not have properly trained everyone. The problems showed up with George faster because he's a bit slower than the others, but I'm afraid the situation could get worse before it gets better unless we look a little deeper into the problem.

Resolving Your Dilemma

The analyses the brothers have just concluded did not solve the problems created by their dilemmas, but they have shown that the quandaries they experienced were probably illusory. Their starting premises, concerning choosing a job and deciding about George, were somewhat spurious. By recognizing that the decision involved more than simply choosing one option or the other—the choices were in fact false—they escaped from their dilemmas (i.e., they went around them). They didn't avoid the issues. Rather, they identified the real problems that they needed to address.

They also illustrated another method for dealing with problems like theirs: Involving other people in a decision makes it much easier to marshal the information you need for grasping the horns of a dilemma—meeting your problem head-on and ensuring that the alternatives you are considering are consistent with the facts and exhaustive. Let's take Tobin's decision, for example. He expresses one part of it this way.

Tobin: If I take the one job, I'll not get ahead as fast as I want; if I can't get ahead as fast as I want, I won't be able to build the house as quickly as I want. Then again, with the other job, I'll probably have to relocate and won't be able to build the house. Either way, I'm stuck.

Sid: I don't think your alternatives are true.

Tobin: What do you mean?

Sid: You can always build your house. If you take the one job, Jane's income can help build it. If you have to take an overseas assignment in the other job, does Jane have to go with you? Couldn't you still build the house and have Jane and the children live in it?

If you have to meet the demands of two or more perspectives at the same time, it's to everyone's advantage to meet them together. That doesn't mean that you can't or shouldn't look at the situation from your own perspective. Unless you inform yourself as to *your* basic issues and *your* problems, you can't discuss them intelligently with anyone else. In a similar vein, the other people affected by the decision need the opportunity to consider *their* options. The final step is then to negotiate a satisfactory resolution to the situation.*

CHAPTER FIVE

Weighing Your Options

❧

In order to inform yourself effectively about what you might really want, you need to weigh your

*See Donald H. Weiss, *Conflict Resolution* (New York: AMA-COM, 1993), or Donald H. Weiss, *Managing Conflict*, a cassette/workbook study program published by the American Management Association, 1992.

options. The fields of sales and management provide us with some simple yet useful tools for making decisions like those we have been discussing: the Ben Franklin close (or weighted analysis) and the decision tree.

The Ben Franklin Close

Salespeople use the Ben Franklin close to help prospective customers make a decision when choosing between the salesperson's products or services and a competitor's. And nothing could be simpler.

First, draw a T-chart. Take a piece of paper (lined notebook paper works best), hold it the long way (eleven inches from top to bottom), and—about two lines or a couple of inches from the top—draw a line from side to side. Then draw a line down the middle of the page, from top to bottom, bisecting the first line. That's a T-chart (there's a sample on page 40). Let's take Tobin's situation to illustrate how to use it.

Tobin: Before I talk to Jane about it, I could run a simple test just to see which of the two positions I really prefer. I may be able to work out some of the difficulties by running a Ben Franklin close on the two of them.

Sid: You've lost me.

Tobin: That's a salesperson's name for a weighted analysis of two competing products or services. Here, give me that pad of paper. I'll draw a T-chart on it and show you how it works. I'll list my two choices and compare them in side-by-side columns by listing each feature or benefit in the columns. Then I'll assign each feature or benefit a point value. I usually use a scale of 1 to 5 when I'm talking with a prospect. I can assign negative values to features that aren't to my advantage. The numbers represent the level of importance or the degree of satisfaction each choice would produce.

Then, after I list all the features and benefits and rate them, I can add up the totals. The side with the higher score or rating is the winner, and I have a pretty good basis for making the decision. Give me a few minutes, and I'll show you what I mean.

Tobin's Ben Franklin close is in Figure 5-1. As you can see, the things that fit in well with his long-term goals and objectives receive the highest ratings. Those that don't receive the lowest ratings, and several items receive negative ratings. When he finishes, he shows his chart to his brother.

Sid: Pretty close scores.
Tobin: Right. It's a tough call.
Sid: Maybe you ought to have Jane do the same thing and then compare scores.
Tobin: That'll help.
Sid: That's assuming she doesn't simply say, "I don't want to leave my job, and I don't want the kids to be uprooted." Then it's a different ballgame.

Figure 5-1. The Ben Franklin close used by Tobin.

Marketing Support Position	Account Executive Position
_5_ Large firm; opportunity for growth	_−1_ Small firm; limited opportunities
_3_ Lower immediate pay	_4_ Higher immediate pay
_5_ Higher potential income	_2_ Slow income growth
_5_ Excellent fringe benefits	_3_ Good fringe benefits
_3_ Small fish in large pond	_2_ Big fish in small pond
_5_ Long-term career	_4_ Stepping stone
_3_ Extensive travel	_4_ Some travel
_3_ Relocation probable	_5_ Relocation improbable
_5_ Status from association with company	_2_ Little recognition out of town
_5_ New experiences for self and family	_5_ Stability in the community
_5_ Educational opportunities	_5_ Roots especially for children
_−2_ Isolation from families	_4_ Close to families
_4_ Children learn languages and cultures	_4_ Children stay in local schools
_3_ Jane has to change gears or stay alone	_5_ Jane maintains career momentum
_−2_ We build house later or Jane does now	_5_ We build new house next year
2 We postpone house	
_2_ I forgo political interests	_5_ I satisfy political interests
_5_ Access to new markets	
59 Total Score	58 Total Score

Tobin: What do you suggest I do then?
Sid: You might try a decision tree.
Tobin: What's that?

Decision Trees

There are several different versions of decision trees. The one I prefer traces the possible consequences of each alternative you are considering. It operates from the premise that "if I do this, then that will happen." (Worst case/best case scenarios are decision trees.) You weight the consequence of the options, and the consequence with the highest score, as in the Ben Franklin close, is the decision. We'll follow Sid's line of reasoning to illustrate the technique.

Sid: I've been thinking of using a decision tree to help me demonstrate to upper management what I think we should do.
Tobin: You're not sure yet?
Sid: To some extent, but I think this decision tree will help solidify my reasoning.
Tobin: Then do it.
Sid: Let's see what happens if I fire George. Now I know this sounds cold, but I'm going to have to limit the consequences to business issues. I can't worry about his family and stuff like that.
Tobin: I didn't say anything.
Sid: I just wanted to head off any appeals to sympathy at a time like this. I have enough doubts based on those factors as it is. So, first . . .

(Now take a look at Sid's tree in Figure 5-2.)

Sid: At best, giving everyone additional training is the least of three evils.

Tobin: If your ratings are accurate.

Sid: Oh, they're somewhat subjective. Yours would be, too, if you ran your options through the same process. That's why we need input from other people. Your situa-

Figure 5-2. A decision tree.

1.	Consequences if I replace George with a new hire.		
	a. Cost of advertising	− 5	
	b. Opportunity costs of interviewing	− 5	
	c. Cost of orientation or training or both	− 5	
	d. Losses during training period	− 2	
	e. Cost in employee morale	− 5	
	f. Losses incurred by not training	− 3	
	g. Gain if new hire works out well	+ 5	− 20
2.	Consequences if I take the time to coach George.		
	a. Time away from my duties	− 2	
	b. Time George away from his	− 2	
	c. Time before he is up to speed	− 2	
	d. Gain if he gets up to speed	+ 5	
	d. Cost if he never gets up to speed	− 5	
	e. Cost of replacing George anyway	− 5*	
	f. Cost in employee morale	− 1	
	g. Losses incurred by not training	− 5	− 17
3.	Consequences if we add training for everyone.		
	a. Time away from my duties	− 2	
	b. Time everyone away from theirs	− 4	
	c. Time before they are all up to speed	− 2	
	d. Gain if they all get up to speed	5	
	d. Cost if George never gets up to speed	− 3	
	e. Cost of replacing George anyway	− 5*	
	f. Cost in employee morale	− 1	− 12

*All values are relative. Whereas the rating of replacing George without trying to help him totals − 20, the relative value of replacing George after training him over everyone is only − 5.

tion may not be as difficult as it seems, and I may be overestimating the cost of replacing George.

Weight Your Options With Iron Bars, Rather Than With Feathers: We could say that Tobin and Sid are weighting their analyses with feathers because their ratings are based on flimsy evidence. To give their weights substance, they, especially Sid, need more substantial data.

Sid can get data from Personnel on the costs of recruiting and training. He can measure the degree to which his work group lacks the skills it needs through testing. He can project the increases in skills as the result of additional training (using figures from the first round of training). He can also get information about the community college program mentioned in Chapter 4 and obtain an agreement from George to get additional training; he can then factor in the cost of tuition reimbursement. In the end, he'll have a solid case to present to top management.

Tobin: What'll you tell your boss tomorrow?
Sid: I'll show him the work we've done here today. He buys into this type of analysis, and he'll give me the extra time to build my case. We've done things like this together before. How about you? What'll you tell your prospective employers?
Tobin: Fortunately, I didn't tell them what time I'd call. Frankly, I don't think it has all that much to do with the *jobs*. I think it's a question of values clarification and nego-

tiation between Jane and me about our future. We have tonight and tomorrow for us to work this out.

Sid: Don't you two have to go to work tomorrow?

Tobin: We're on vacation.

Tobin was right a while back when he said he should have attacked this decision in consultation with Jane before this. Still, they have the opportunity to grapple with the issues before it's too late.

And Sid is fortunate to have a receptive manager. He really needed to have a dialogue with his boss long before this, but it's not too late for him, either.

With the proper tools, making a reasoned decision on the basis of solid information becomes much easier—regardless of how tough the decision seems.

Conclusion

❧

Making the tough decisions is never easy—even with the good advice of this book. Emotional issues, on which we barely touched, are rarely decided by purely rational means. Once you hit on the nerve of values, you tread upon emotions and feelings. Choosing to let George go or to uproot Tobin's family isn't just a cut-and-dried business decision unless you choose to dehumanize the lives of the people involved.

In the end, Sid may have to fire George. Tobin may have to choose the job that would require relocation. They will then have to deal with their own feelings, as well as with those of the other people. But by having completed these analyses—seeking out the basic issues, identifying the real problems, and weighing options—they will have at least cut through the clouds obscuring the situation. Involving other people in making these decisions will help them sell the outcomes, because the decisions will be as much the others' as Tobin's or Sid's.

Making tough decisions is never easy, but you can make it *easier* by following this basic principle of self-management: manage your situation before problems become crises.

What Drives Me?

∽

Anything you do, you do for a reason, even if you don't know what that reason is. Every action produces an end result, and, unless you plan carefully, the end result you get may not satisfy the

This appendix was adapted from Donald H. Weiss, "What Drives You to Work?" (Dallas: Self-Management Associates, 1982), a self-evaluation instrument included in the cassette-workbook program "Getting Results: The Performance Appraisal Process" and in *Managing Stress* (New York: AMACOM, 1985, 1987).

reason for which you took the action in the first place.

Some reasons compel you more than others. We call such reasons motives, and we can trace them back to needs or wants. The reasons that motivate you most forcefully are your drivers—your most important reasons for doing what you're doing. Satisfying those drivers becomes your most important activity because reaching those goals means getting the payoffs you want for yourself. So what are your drivers?

The list below contains twenty-five possible reasons for doing anything. Each word or phrase can be used to answer the question "What do I want to get out of the effort I'm putting into my life?"

Instructions

This is important. Read the *entire* list of possible payoffs before continuing. Stop here and read the list.

___ 1. *KNOWLEDGE*: To pursue and learn about new things and ideas; to search for truth or information; to be known by others as an intelligent person and to feel intelligent.

___ 2. *WISDOM*: To understand and frame for myself a meaning of life, perceiving experience from a broad frame of reference.

___ 3. *POWER*: To lead and direct others; to influence or control others—that is, to get them to do what I want them to do.

___ 4. *AESTHETIC PLEASURE*: To enjoy and respect the things from which I derive pleasure—art, nature, work, people.

___ 5. *ETHICAL STANDARDS*: To believe in and maintain a code of ethics, a sense of right and wrong; to be moral; to conform to the standards of society, my family or spouse, my profession, and my personal or religious ideals.

___ 6. *INDEPENDENCE*: To achieve my own goals in the manner best suited to me; to have freedom to come and go as I wish; to be myself at all times; to control my own actions.

___ 7. *ACCOMPLISHMENT*: To achieve my personal objectives with a sense that I've done something as well as, if not better than, someone else would have; to experience self-satisfaction when I rise to a challenge, accomplish a task or a job, or solve a problem.

___ 8. *RECOGNITION*: To receive attention, notice, approval, or respect from others because of something I've done; to generate a feeling of respect in others for who I am and what I achieve.

___ 9. *FRIENDSHIP*: To have many friends; to work with others, enjoying their companionship; to join groups for companionship; to look forward to and to enjoy social relations.

___10. *RESPONSIBILITY*: To be held accountable to others or to organizations to which I belong for a job or task; to possess something and care for it.

___11. *CREATIVITY*: To be free to and to have the ability and desire to develop new ideas, solutions to problems, improvements in products or procedures, or designs of things or plans; to be challenged intellectually; to be first, to innovate or create.

___12. *SECURITY*: To possess the basic wherewithal for living; to feel safe; to have self-confidence; to have job security and continuity of income.

___13. *DEDICATION*: To be loyal to the company or my supervisor, my family, social and political groups, and others; to give devotion, commitment, or friendship to others.

___14. *JUSTICE AND PARITY*: To receive rewards and recognition for my contributions and achievements in proportion to my effort and comparable to those received by other people.

___15. *GROWTH*: To advance, to expand my life through my job or through the improvement of my status at work or in the community; to increase my work- and non-work-related knowledge or skill; to find fulfillment in the groups in which I work or live; to mature personally and professionally.

___16. *SELF-ESTEEM*: To be someone of value in my own eyes and in the eyes of other people; to be accepted as a person, rather than as a nonentity or as a means to an end; to feel useful and wanted by other people; to be a leader; to be appreciated by others.

___17. *RELIGIOUSNESS*: To believe in a supreme

being; to relate to others on a spiritual or personal basis with respect to some faith or set of beliefs.

___18. *LOVE*: To experience warmth, feelings of affection, a sense of caring, and enthusiasm for, attachment to, devotion to, and interest in something or in another person, especially someone to whom I can make a commitment.

___19. *CHALLENGE*: To feel good about what I do, its degree of difficulty, and the complexity or demands on my creativity; to have opportunities to apply my knowledge and skills effectively and easily.

___20. *FAITH*: To have self-confidence and to believe in my abilities and skills, in the goodness and value of life, and in the goals and objectives of my company or social organizations; to feel secure in the availability of help from others and to recognize help received.

___21. *HELPFULNESS*: To provide assistance, support, empathy, or protection to others; to be open, responsive, and generous.

___22. *HEALTH (PHYSICAL/MENTAL)*: To feel energetic and free of physical pain from injury, disease, or infection; to feel free of worry and anxiety and of emotional blocks to success in all aspects of my life; to have peace of mind.

___23. *MONEY*: To have sufficient income or other assets to use as I wish; to be materially comfortable or well off.

___24. *GOOD TIMES/PLEASURE*: To have fun; to

enjoy myself; to do things I like to do rather than only things I have to do.

___25. *BEING LOVED*: To experience warmth, feelings of affection, and a sense of caring from other people, especially from someone from whom I can expect a commitment.

Now return to the beginning of the list. Slowly review each item, ranking each payoff according to its importance to you. In the spaces provided, write 1 for the most important and 25 for the least. For example, if you feel that knowledge is important but not the most important reason for doing things, you might write an 8 on the first line. It may make things easier if you hunt out the item that represents the most important reason before you rate the rest.

Turn to the next steps only after you have finished the previous step.

Figure A-1. A model chart of drivers.

Rank	Work-Related Drivers	Rank	Nonwork-Related Drivers
2	Recognition	1	Love
4	Friendship	3	Being loved
5	Accomplishment	4	Friendship
15	Money	20	Religiousness
9	Responsibility	8	Aesthetic pleasure

Using Figure A-1 as a guide, transfer the top five payoffs you want from your *work* from your master list to the chart in Figure A-2. For example, you might list recognition as the most important work-related driver, even if it ranks lower than that on your master list. Then list the five *personal* payoffs you most want to satisfy outside the workplace. These drivers help you maintain your psychological well-being and your social relationships.

When you complete your list of payoffs in each group, compare the two lists. Note which side of the chart—work-related or nonwork-related—contains the highest ratings in the master list.

In some cases, payoffs may be both work- and nonwork-related. For example, many people seek friendship at work, as well as outside of work. As Figure A-1 shows, you can list a driver on both sides of the chart.

When you finish, you'll have a personal pro-

Figure A-2. *Your* drivers.

Rank	Work-Related Drivers	Rank	Nonwork-Related Drivers

file, a picture of your own most important motives or reasons for doing things. Check your lists of payoffs to see which of them you think you should pursue most vigorously. The decisions you make should fit with these goals. Unless you integrate your goals, you may feel a great deal of frustration and stress.

Suggested Readings

❧

Argyris, Chris. "Interpersonal Barriers to Decision Making." *Harvard Business Review* (January–February 1991): pp. 121–134.

———. *Reasoning, Learning, and Action: Individual and Organizational.* San Francisco: Jossey-Bass, 1982.

Hill, Norman C. *Increasing Managerial Effectiveness: Keys to Management and Motivation.* Reading, Mass.: Addison-Wesley, 1979.

Vroom, Victor, and Philip Yetton. *Leadership and Decision-Making.* Pittsburgh: University of Pittsburgh, 1973.

Weiss, Donald H. *Get Organized! How to Control Your Life Through Self-Management.* New York: AMACOM, 1986.

Weiss, Donald H., and Randy Wilp. *Get Organized! for Windows: The Goal-Driven Personal and Performance Manager for Busy People.* St. Louis: Self-Management Communications, 1992.

Index

∽

[Page numbers in italics represent figures.]

About the Author

❧

Donald H. Weiss, Ph.D., is CEO of Self-Management Communications, Inc., St. Louis, and a well-known author of books, videos, and cassette-workbook programs that focus on management and interpersonal skills. He has been a senior training and development executive and consultant for more than twenty-five years. Among his corporate positions were: program manager for the Citicorp Executive Development Center and corporate training manager for Millers' Mutual Insurance. His many publications include fifteen previous books in the SOS series and *Fair, Square, and Legal: Safe Hiring, Managing, and Firing Practices to Keep Your Company Out of Court* (all AMACOM). Dr. Weiss earned his Ph.D. from Tulane University.